CAMOUFLAGE & M

Royal Air Force 1939~1945

Compiled by

Mike Reynolds

Assisted by
Bernie McCartney

Argus Books

ARGUS BOOKS
Argus House
Boundary Way
Hemel Hempstead
Herts HP2 7ST
England

First published by Argus Books 1992
© Argus Books 1992

ISBN 1 85486 065 8

Phototypesetting by
Island Graphics, Chesham.
Printed and bound in Great Britain by William
Clowes Ltd., Beccles.

Publisher's Note
During the printing process, the roundels
on the back cover of this book appear black.
The true colour is Roundel Blue.

Introduction

I T IS not the intention of this book to give an in-depth appraisal of the technical details, nor a concise history or performance analysis of the various aircraft illustrated. There are far more qualified people who have already covered this area of research in many other volumes, some in great detail.

My purpose is to draw and describe for the modeller some of the most modelled aircraft of World War Two, giving a good basic set of information on the so-called standard colours and markings set out by the various Government departments controlling aircraft production. There were, of course, thousands of variations, deviations and other oddities brought about by the vagaries of wear and tear in the front line and even training units, the difficulties of war-time production, repair and supply, or in some instances simple variations brought about by the personal preferences of individuals or units.

In many cases, aircraft units and sometimes pilots can be identified by such markings and badges whilst, in some notable cases, individual units are identifiable by their own modifications to the issued camouflaged machines.

You can see, therefore, that this small volume can only provide a base of limited data for a selected few aircraft, although I hope that the modeller, whether working on static solid scale and plastic or flying scale models, will be able to produce a presentable representative miniature from the information found here. However, for specific subjects there can be no substitution for in-depth, detailed and cross-referenced research, especially in reference to good quality photographs which are to be found in many magazines and books specialising on specific periods, air forces, campaigns, and aircraft. These can often be quite costly, so a visit to your local library is recommended.

I often find cheap books on aircraft on stalls at airshows, whilst a visit to your local model shop could prove fruitful, and friends are often a good source. However, beware of relying too much on line drawing and artwork, some of which is highly dubious, especially that which was produced some years ago, whilst many scale drawings, even recent productions, have inaccuracies. In fact, accurate drawings are quite rare.

When consulting your colour photographs, it must be kept in mind that the accurate reproduction from some film emulsions of the period is not as good as that produced by modern technology, whilst others have deteriorated with age. Varying light conditions also have dramatic results on the published product, as can frequently be seen in currently published periodicals. There is the renowned example of a squadron of Mustangs, long thought of as painted blue on their upper surfaces, which actually turned out to be standard olive green on research and correction in the reproduction. Memory can be just as fallible. For instance, the example of the P51 Mustang 'Milli G', which the pilot recalled painted scarlet and which was produced in kit form to reflect this was later found to have been finished in the standard olive drab finish. However, modern technology and research have made great improvements in elimination of these errors and I hope the colour chips and drawings will help you in producing a more accurate finish.

One last consideration in this modelling minefield is that of scale colour. With the distance between the viewer and the subject increasing, the actual intensity of colour pales. This phenomenon has long been exploited by the artist, especially in landscape painting, to give a sense of depth to the work. A school of thought in modelling circles believes that the discipline in art should be applied to modelling work. A 1/72nd scale model viewed at the optimum distance of 12" represents looking at a full-size object at a distance of about 100ft. It should, according to this school of thought, be paler in colour than if the object is viewed at a close distance. The recommended colour mix is quoted as 40% white to 60% basic colour to give a representative toned down hue, whilst for other scales the proportions of white to colour must be adjusted accordingly, but the results are entirely to the liking of the builder. Experiment a little until you find a finish that is pleasing to you, and balance this with a little wear and tear weathering for the final acceptable result.

Gloster Gladiator

The Gloster Gladiator was the last of the RAF's fighter biplanes although, as such, it introduced the latest innovations of an enclosed cockpit and flaps on the lower wings. It was already obsolete when World War Two was declared, but a hard-pressed, RAF in the midst of re-equipping was forced to provide the type as front line equipment, along with early Hurricanes, to the British Expeditionary Forces.

After the fall of France, it was used as a second line fighter on fields too small for the new monoplane Spitfires and Hurricanes. The Gladiator was also to soldier on for some time with the Royal Navy and in the Middle East and Mediterranean theatres of war where it gained glory in the defence of Malta in 1941.

Several Sea Gladiators stored in crates there were taken over by the RAF to form the island's defence flight, and were immortalised as 'Faith, Hope & Charity' although, in fact, there were more than three aircraft and the amount of enemy air raids was somewhat less than legend would now have us believe.

The three-view drawing shows the type in typical 1940 colour scheme, and is interesting in that it shows the tops of the lower wings in lighter shades of green and Dark Earth to compensate for shadow. However, while this was laid down as standard, it is believed to have been the exception rather than the rule, whilst the undersides varied from the pre-War silver, through a black/white scheme, to the standard blue undersurfaces.

The small, adjacent sketches show the doped silver, and flamboyant squadron markings of the pre-War era. The second side view shows the aircraft hastily re-painted into drab camouflage during the Munich Crisis. At this time, many aircraft were seen only bearing type 'B' red/blue national marking on the fuselage side, with none on the top wing, but in some cases retaining full marking on the underside of the lower wings.

The third side illustration shows the Gladiator in Mediterranean theatre colours, where a stone colour replaced dark green and the more intense Azure Blue, more suited to hot sky environment, replaced the paler 'sky' blue on the undersides.

The final side view shows the aircraft in its Malta Sea Gladiator colour scheme, with Dark Slate Grey and Dark Sea Grey upper surface to the same basic pattern as shown in the three-view drawing with Sky type 'S' undersurface.

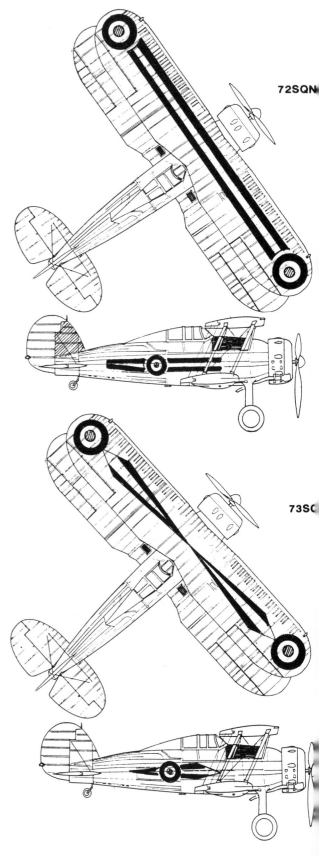

72SQN

73SQ

PRE-WAR SQUADRON MARKINGS

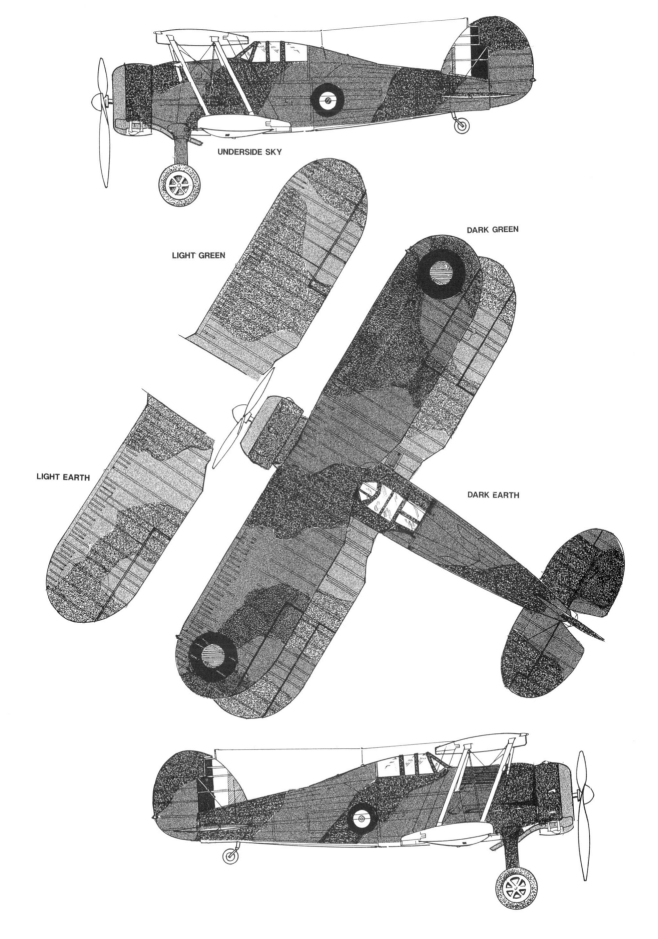

UNDERSIDE SKY

LIGHT GREEN

DARK GREEN

LIGHT EARTH

DARK EARTH

Hawker Hurricane

The Hurricane was the most numerous fighter type in the Royal Air Force's inventory at the outbreak of war and during the subsequent Battle of Britain, when the type accounted for more enemy aircraft shot down than all the other defences combined. The Hurricane was the link between the then traditionally-built framework and fabric construction and the newly developed monocoque, all-metal stressed structures, which was used in the Spitfire and Messerschmitt 109. Despite being outclassed by these aircraft, it was the traditional basis of construction that gave the aircraft its initial advantages of being more easy to build, repair, and fly, and its wide, inward-closing undercarriage gave it far superior ground handling. This was an important factor for the fresh-from-training-school novice pilots who were committed into battle in 1940.

The three-view drawing shows the aircraft in its Battle of Britain scheme, with the small underside views giving some idea of the development of colours during this early period of conflict. When one wing was painted black, the ailerons were often left in their original colour so as not to upset the balance of these control surfaces.

The top side view again shows a pre-War aircraft from III Squadron based at Northolt, with doped silver undersides bearing the serial numbers as shown in the small sketches.

Side view number two shows an aircraft serving with the ill-fated British Expeditionary Force, with fin markings applied in the French style to facilitate international recognition. Many of these aircraft were early production aircraft with fabric covered wings and wooden two-blade propellers.

The third view shows an aircraft serving in Russia with 151 Wing and consequently bearing Russian Air Force style individual markings. These aircraft were left behind for use by the Russian Allies on the Wing's return and subsequently re-marked with the 'Red' stars of that nation.

Side view four shows the transition from defence to offence, with the colours changing from Green/Earth and Sky Blue to Dark Grey/Green upper surfaces with Light Grey undersides. In late 1940, a 18" wide band of Sky type S was added just forward of the tail to aid recognition.

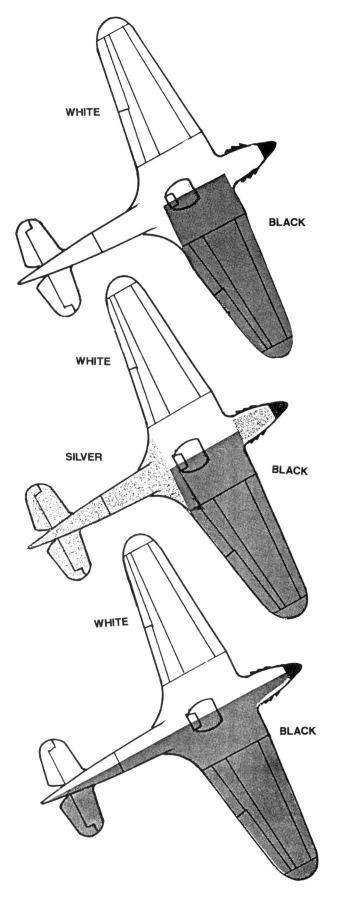

WHITE

BLACK

WHITE

SILVER

BLACK

WHITE

BLACK

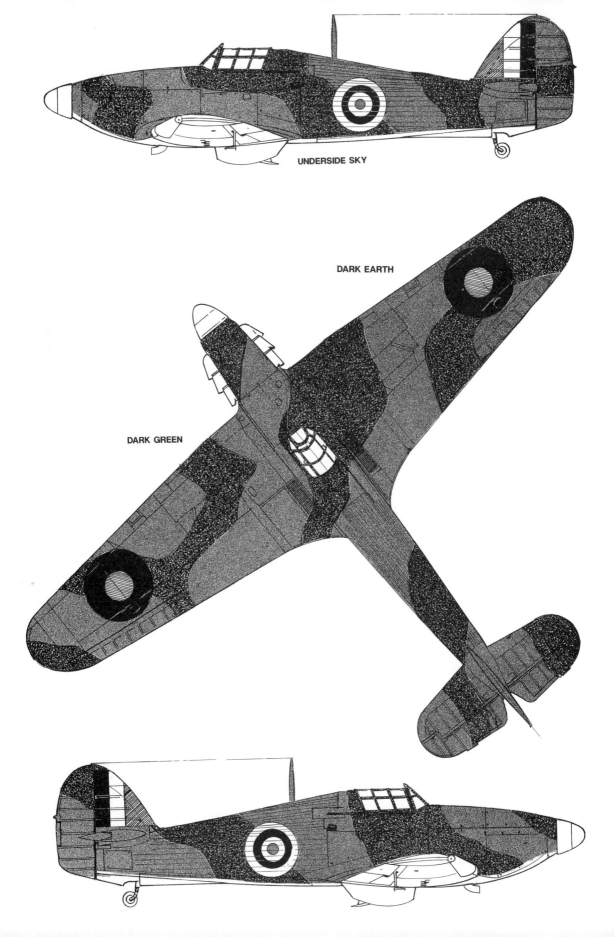

UNDERSIDE SKY

DARK EARTH

DARK GREEN

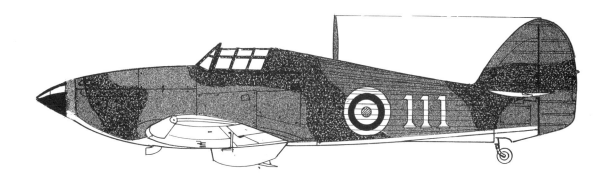

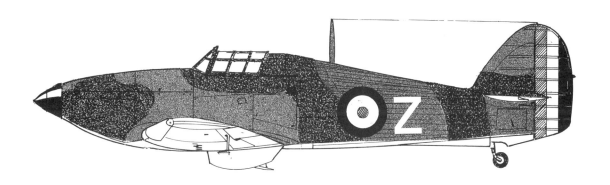

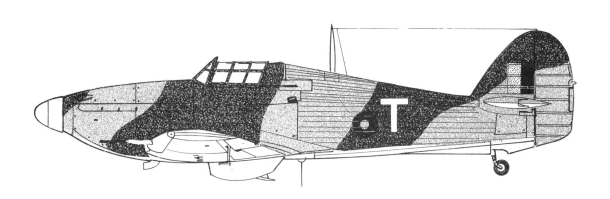

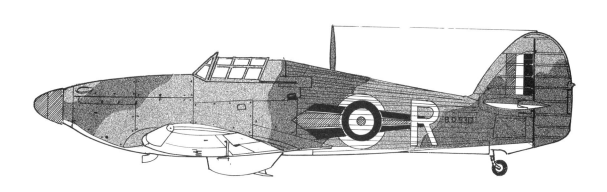

Fairey Swordfish

Introduced into Royal Naval service in 1936, this big biplane was by the outbreak of War in '39 an anachronism, much of its design, manufacturing methods, and certainly its performance with a cruising speed of approx 90 knots, belonging to an earlier era if not an earlier war. Nevertheless, because Great Britain did not have the resources, nor the time to build carriers capable of operating the new, faster monoplane types then on the drawing board, the Swordfish was destined not only to enter the war, but to serve throughout!

This was somewhat justified by its initial success, when a small mixed force of torpedo and bomb-carrying Swordfish seriously crippled the Italian fleet at the port of Taranto. The aircraft's service, however, was not without setback, and even tragedy, such as when the entire unit of six aircraft was lost when trying to intercept the German fleet sailing through the channel.

The three views show the basic style of camouflage introduced at the opening of the conflict and subsequently continually modified to meet operational requirements.

The first of the side views shows the type in pre-War markings, with a silver doped finish, surmounted by red, white, blue national markings, black serials under the wings and unit designation colour bands diagonally applied round the rear fuselage bearing the aircraft call sign number in white. This particular machine is one of seventy float plane examples built to operate as spotter/communication aircraft, and catapult-launched from Battleships and cruiser warships or shore installations.

The second side view shows an aircraft operating against the *Bismarck* breakout in the North Atlantic, with the underside 'Sky' colour extended well up the fuselage sides.

The third view shows an aircraft in the revised Dark Slate Grey/Dark Sea Grey topsides and White sides and bottom surfaces as seen in 1944. Aircraft in the North European theatre also carried the Black and White invasion stripes.

The fourth example shows an aircraft operated by the Royal Air Force as an invasion and supply line protection aircraft, carrying air-to-surface search ASV Mk X radar, and finished in Night Black camouflage to suit its nocturnal role.

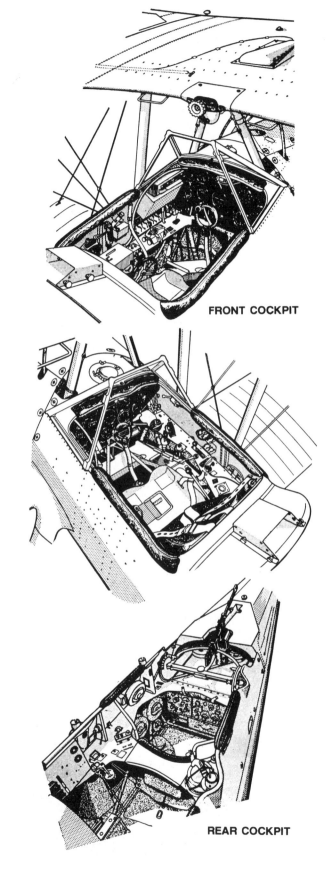

FRONT COCKPIT

REAR COCKPIT

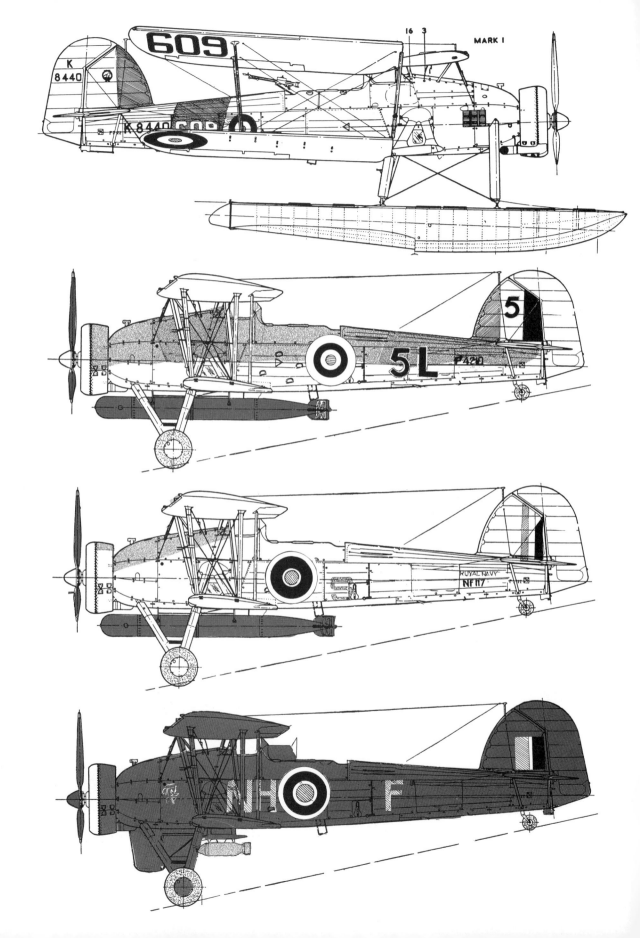

Boulton Paul Defiant

The Defiant, after an initial blaze of success over the beaches of Dunkirk, where the British Expeditionary Force and its French allies were trapped by rapidly-advancing German forces, was not a great success. The Me109e bomber escort pilots mistook the type for Hurricanes, and attacked in line astern right into the fire from the four Browning machine guns. They were not to make that mistake again, and the two Squadrons committed into conflict in the Battle of Britain were both rapidly decimated, and their remnants rapidly withdrawn to less active areas.

Only the change in German tactics in October 1940 from daylight raids to night bombing missions saw the Defiant return to action as an interim night fighter, a role it continued to fill until finally replaced by more suitable twin-engined types from mid-1941 through to mid-1942, when it was relegated to Air Sea Rescue and target towing duties.

The top view shows the CO's aircraft of 264 Squadron in its standard daytime finish just before it was lost in August 1940. The aircraft has Sky Blue under sides, without national markings. The second view shows a night fighter from 256 Squadron in April 1941. It is finished in very matt black RDM2a finish with grey codes and standard A1 fuselage roundels. The B type wing top markings had a lighter blue shade than normal.

In March 1942, the type was introduced into Air Sea Rescue Service. The camouflage was applied in the temperate Dark Slate Grey over extra Dark Sea Grey in the B pattern, with Sky type S undersides. Ultimately, five squadrons filled this role.
The final view for this type shows the aircraft in its final role as a target-towing tug, painted in broad alternate, yellow and black diagonal stripes for obvious reasons!

POLAND

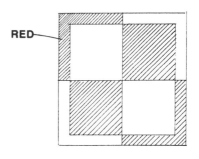

RED

FRANCE

HOLLAND

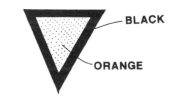

BLACK

ORANGE

GREEK

LIGHT BLUE

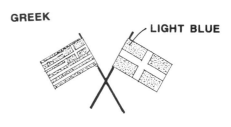

CZECHOSLOVAKIA

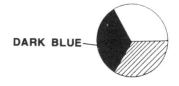

DARK BLUE

NATIONAL MARKINGS BORNE BY R.A.F. AIRCRAFT TO DENOTE CREW OR SQUADRON ORIGIN

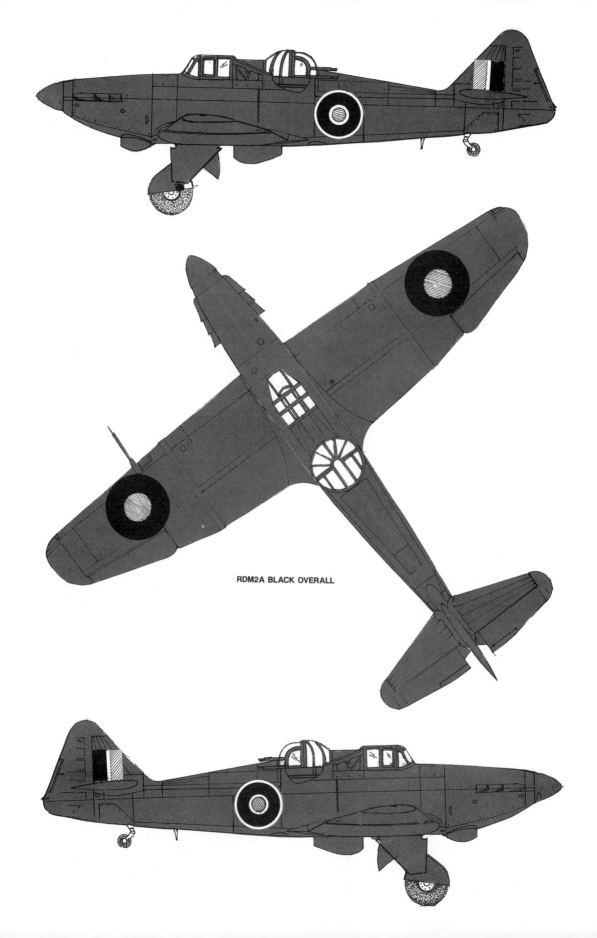

RDM2A BLACK OVERALL

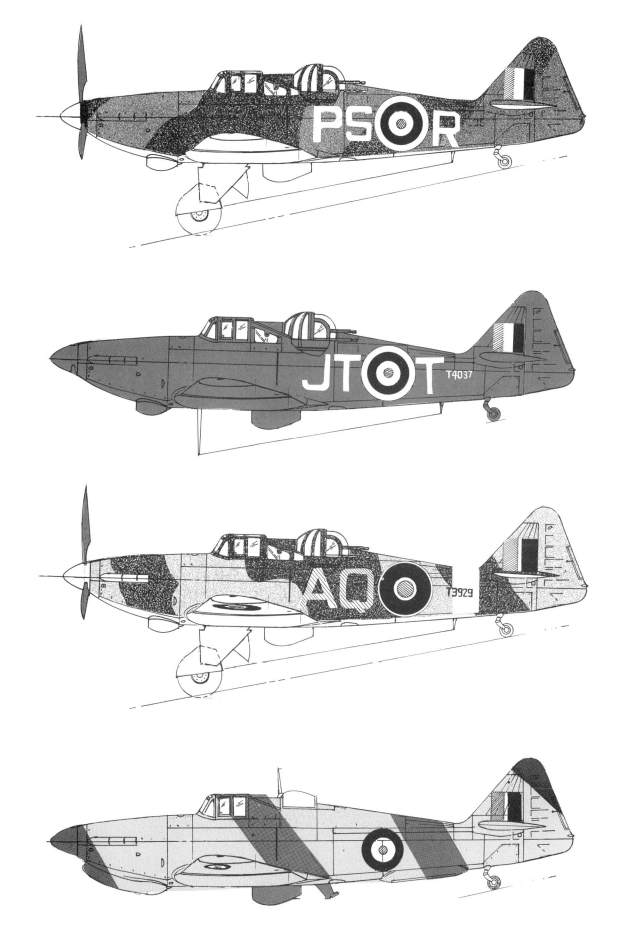

The Supermarine Spitfire

This aircraft is the most famous combat aircraft of the Second World War.

Although it was almost continually matched, or even bettered, by its opponents, it remained a firm favourite with its pilots. It was once described by Douglas Bader as an 'extension of the crewman', reflecting instantly his slightest whim. To the British public, it was the symbol of their lone resistance and was immortalised as such in a dozen films and hundreds of books, and it literally became a legend in its own time. It served in almost every theatre of the War and was used by most of the Allied Air Forces, including the Russians and the Americans.

Basically unsuitable for the role, the Spitfire was adapted for naval warfare as the Seafire, but its light structure and narrow tracked undercarriage made landing and deck handling a continuing difficulty. This type was the last to see combat in the Korean War.

The three-view drawing shows the basic camouflage pattern which was used throughout the aircraft's service, although the colours changed in 1941 and again for naval use. This pattern could be applied either as shown, or in a mirror image. It was intended to be applied alternately to odd and even numbered airframes, but photographic evidence indicates it was more likely to be applied by the production batch.

The first side view is a Mark II in the Dark Earth/Dark Green/Sky undersurface scheme used for the defensive role in 1940 during the Battle of Britain and for a short time afterwards. When the RAF went over to the offensive, the brown was seen to be unsuitable for operations over a grey-green Channel sea and was replaced by a Dark Sea Grey colour and the underside Sky Blue by Light Grey, as is shown on the second view which is the Mark V variant.

The Mk IX proved to be the most successful of all the marks, fullfilling many roles, such as long-range bomber escort, ground attack and, as illustration three shows, in a photographic role. This aircraft is, in fact, finished in an overall pink colour, a scheme previously seen on PR MkIs and MkIV machines.

High altitude fighters had their own colours initially, with a PRU Blue upper surface and Deep Sky Blue underside later changed to a Light Grey upper surface and PRU undersurfaces.

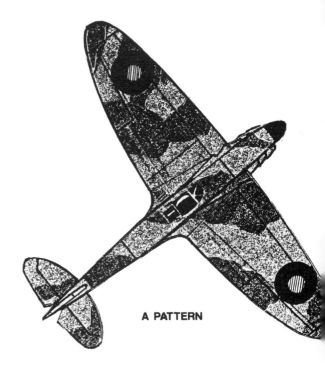

A PATTERN

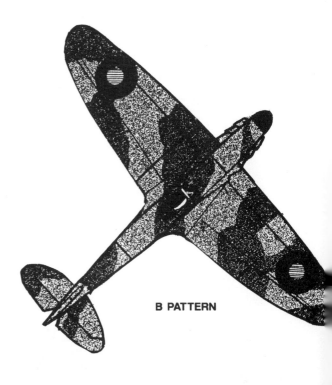

B PATTERN

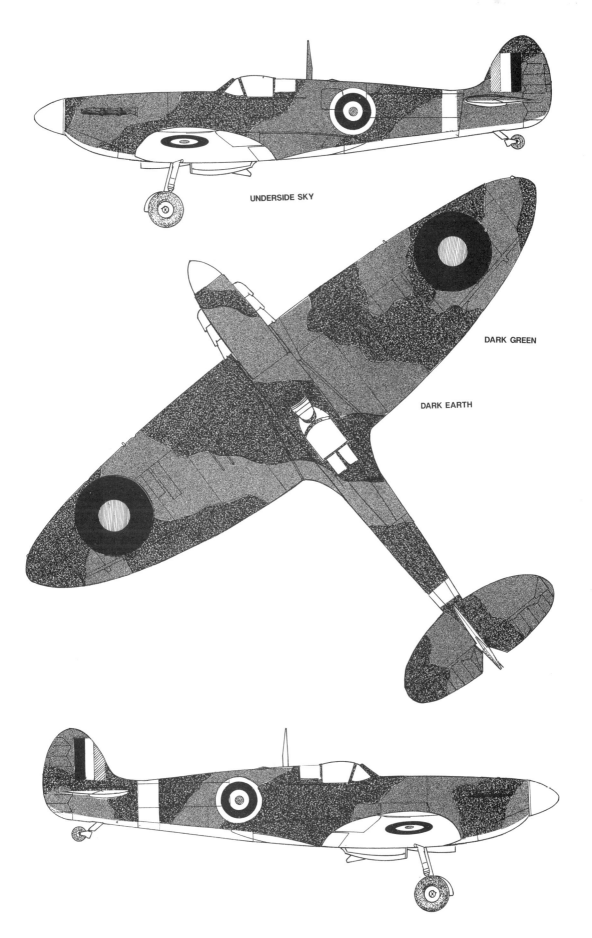

UNDERSIDE SKY

DARK GREEN

DARK EARTH

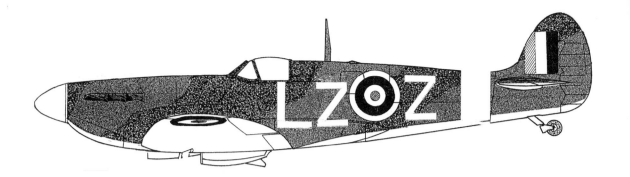

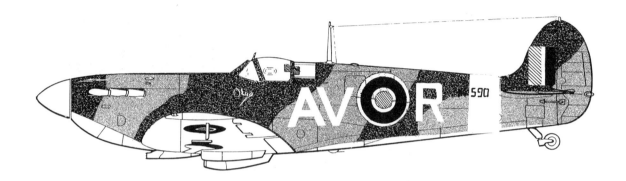

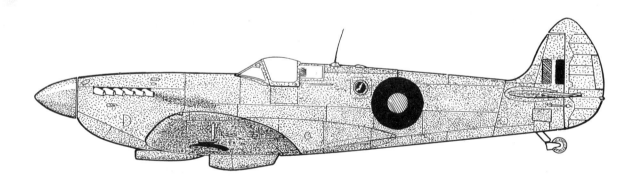

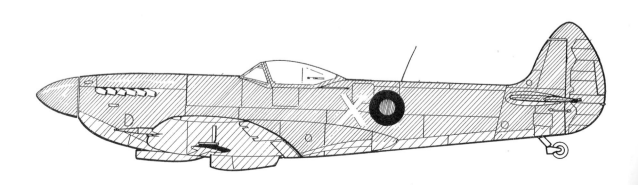

Westland Whirlwind

The Whirlwind made its maiden flight from Boscombe Down on 11th October 1938. It could have been an outstanding combat aircraft, but it was based on two Rolls-Royce Peregrine engines and, as Britain was concentrating on producing the more proven single engine types, the Hurricane and Spitfire, Rolls-Royce concentrated their efforts on the more successful Merlin engine, to the detriment of the Westland machine, which was to be produced in relatively small numbers. It saw only limited service, even when such a type used as a long-range intrusion and escort fighter would have been most useful during the later air offensives.

The three views show the type's standard pattern based on the RAF original scheme, with 28in dia type A1 national markings on the fuselage sides, and type B Red/Blue markings on the wing upper surfaces.

The top view shows an early production aircraft in service with 263 Fighter Squadron during August 1940, while under service acceptance. Note the broad 8" fin stripes extending the full height. The brown/green fuselage camouflage wraps entirely round the fuselage, with the underside of the port wing black and the starboard white, both bearing type A Red, White and Blue cockades.

The second view shows the revision introduced on 27th November 1940, with shortened fin stripes and the recognition aids of an 18" Sky coloured band around the rear fuselage and similar coloured spinners.

In August 1941, yet another revised scheme came into use (view three), introducing a mixed grey, of seven parts of Medium Sea Grey to one part Night Black, or Ocean Grey replacing the dark Earth top colour. A Medium Sea Grey replaced the Sky Blue undersurfaces, which had themselves replaced the black/white scheme from late June 1940. (This single colour had, in turn, been modified by the application of a semi-permanent black distemper to the port wing which lasted from November 1940 to April 1941.)

The fourth view shows the final changes, with the introduction of type C and C1 roundels replacing the old A and A1 markings on the wing undersides and fuselage, and fin flash with narrow 2" White stripe.The aircraft also bears the Yellow strips outboard of the engine nacelles on the wing leading edges and tapering from 5" inboard to 2 1/2" at the tips.

AIR COMMODORE

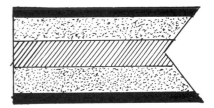

GROUP CAPTAIN

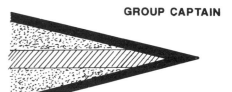

WING COMMANDER

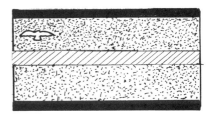

SQUADRON LEADER

**RANK BADGES APPLIED TO THE SIDES
PERSONAL AIRCRAFT**

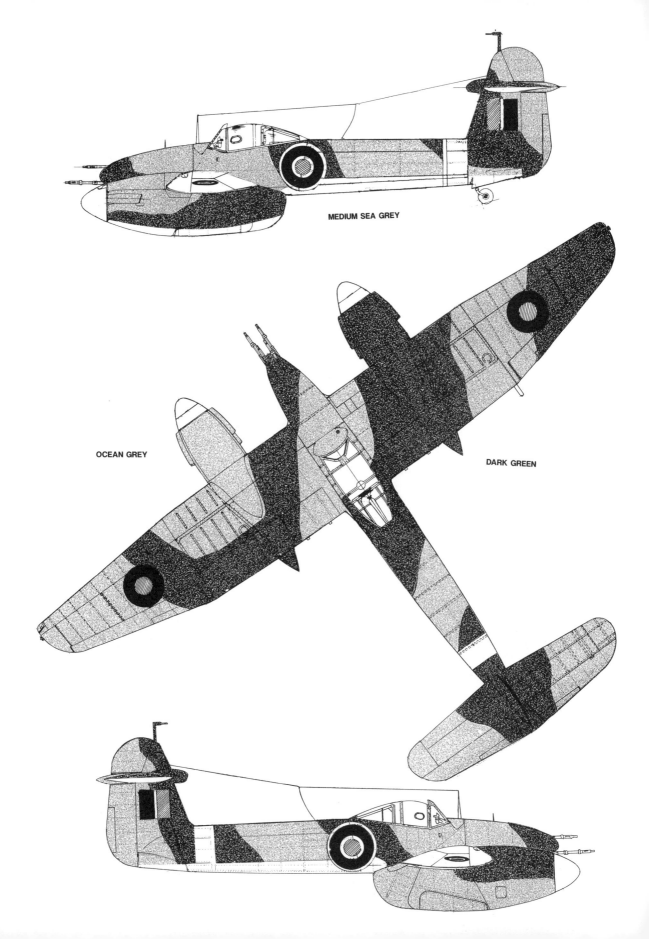

MEDIUM SEA GREY

OCEAN GREY

DARK GREEN

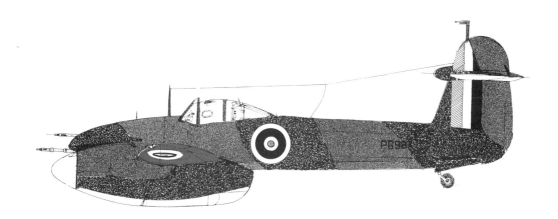

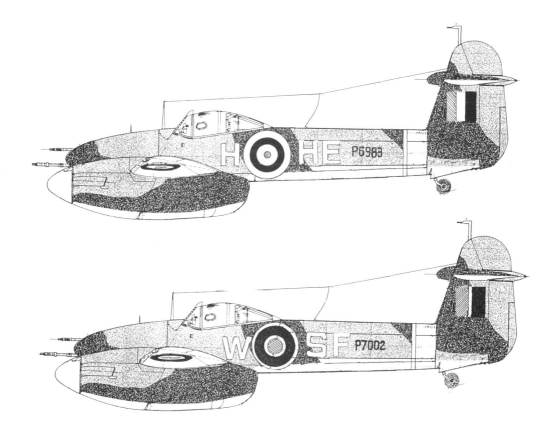

Armstrong Whitworth Whitley

There were many unprepossessing aircraft on both sides of the conflict, whose unglamorous simple workman-like shape gave them little appeal. None more so than the Whitley which, nose-down, slogged doggedly into enemy skies night after night giving the British civilian the feeling that we were still able 'To give back as good as we got'.

The Whitley was, in fact, the only heavy bomber the British had at the beginning of the war, the Hampden and Wellington being officially classed as medium bombers. For all its modesty, it was also able to chalk up many firsts and, although it was designed to a specification some two years after that which produced the Hampden and Wellington, it entered service some time before, taking only 20 months from contract to service. It was the first to drop bombs on German soil, the first to bomb Berlin and the first to attack Italy. It also bore the brunt of the night offensive for the first years of the War when aircraft were sent out singly, plotting their own routes and times to hit specific targets, such as factories and railway stations, and to bring their bombs back if they could not be sure of not hitting civilian residences, and all this by dead reckoning. No wonder only some 5% of bombs dropped during this period were anywhere near targets while some 50% were over a mile out!

This should not detract, however, from the courage of the crews or the ability and record of this 'unsung' workhorse.

The four views show the aircraft in the colour scheme used while the aircraft was used for long range patrols with Coastal Command with extra Dark Sea Grey and Dark Slate Grey topsides.

Top view shows the aircraft in early war bombing colours while serving with 10 Squadron from Dishforth. Some aircraft were finished in overall black during 1941 as shown in the second side view.

The third view shows the aircraft in grey/green temperate land finish used while leaflet and supply dropping over occupied Europe. The final side view shows an aircraft used for training British parachute troops and, unusually, having an overall brown colour fuselage but retaining green/brown wing top surfaces and black undersides.

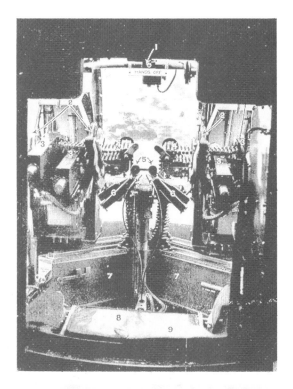

REAR TURRET DETAIL

22

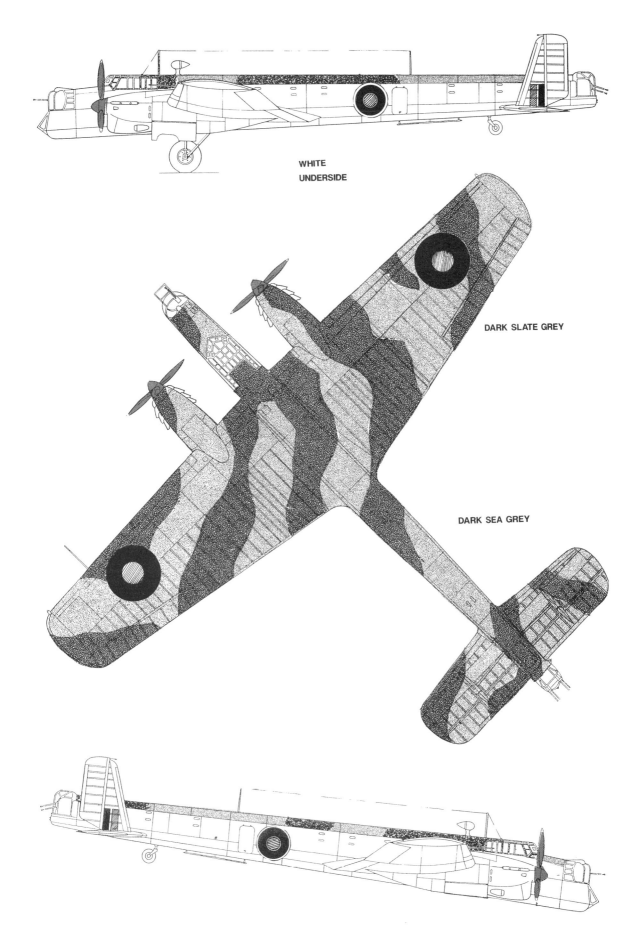

WHITE
UNDERSIDE

DARK SLATE GREY

DARK SEA GREY

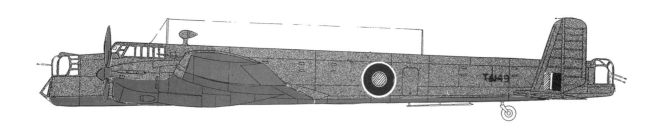

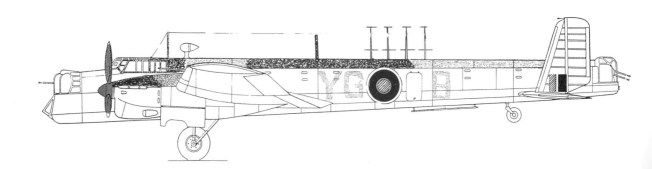

The Bristol Blenheim

One of the several British types to perform well into the War in continuous, unstinting, but unspectacular work was the Blenheim, which was almost the only type to take a daylight bombing offensive into the hostile skies of Europe.

It also served with honour, if not distinction, during the British withdrawal from Greece and again in operations over the deserts of North Africa and the jungles of Asia.

When the bomber was introduced, it caused a sensation, being some 25mph faster than the standard RAF day fighter of the time. It was then logical to develop a long-range escort fighter.

Both Mark 1 and Mark IV variants were adapted in this way, the former being one of the first aircraft to carry the AI airborne radar with limited results.

The first side view shows a Mk1 bomber as seen at the outbreak of War in the autumn of 1939. Serving with 90 Squadron, this machine bears a standard AI roundel on the fuselage side, hastily modified at Squadron level to give a toned-down effect similar to the Standard B type.

The second view shows the modified fighter version in the matt black RDF2 finish, which had a very sooty appearance. Unfortunately, this paint did not wear well, with poor adhesion and marking on the slightest pretext. It was also reported to have slowed the aircraft down by some 15mph through skin friction. This finish, beside being unpopular, was also compromised by the large A1 fuselage markings and light Grey Squadron codes.

Third view is of the MkII bomber in standard day colours of the Green/Dark Earth upper surfaces and Sky undersides. This mark would also be seen in temperate Dark Sea Grey/Slate Grey top sides when serving with Coastal Command and Stone/Dark Earth top and Azure undersides when serving in North Africa.

Mark V was not a success and had only a short service career service operating in India and the Far East during 1942/43 and Italy, where losses became unacceptably high. The aircraft shown served with 8 Squadron in anti-shipping sorties over the Red Sea and is finished in the two Grey temperate scheme with White undersides extending well up the fuselage sides.

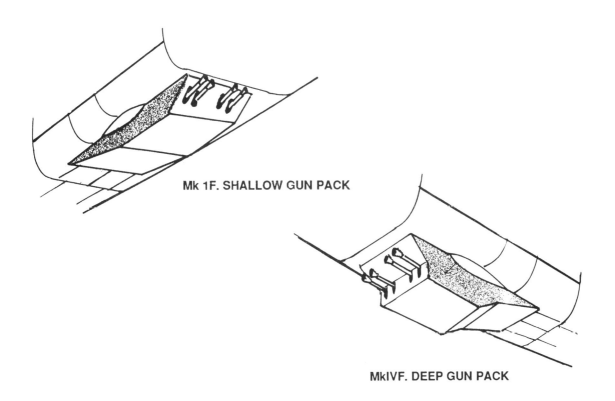

Mk 1F. SHALLOW GUN PACK

MkIVF. DEEP GUN PACK

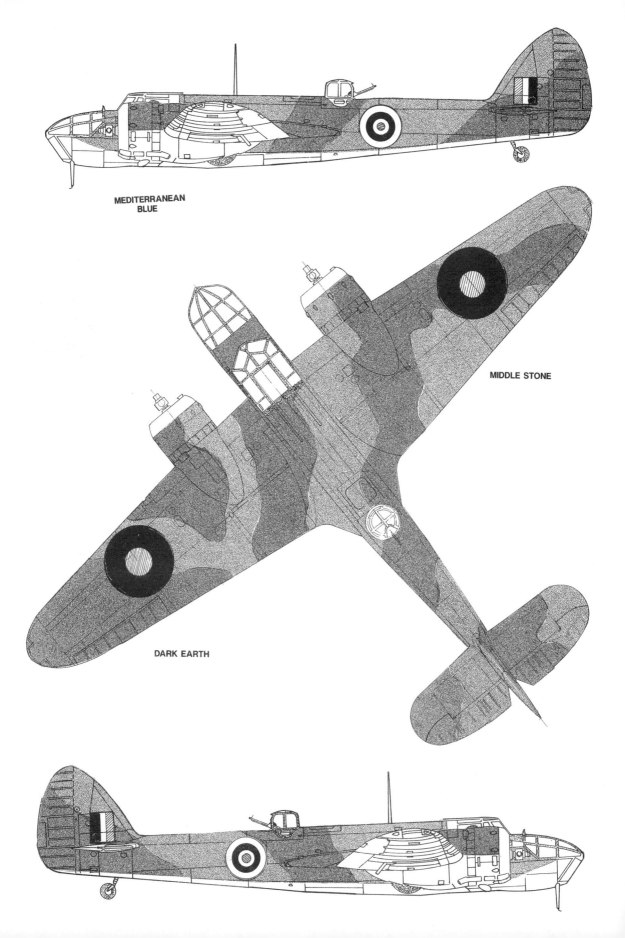

MEDITERRANEAN
BLUE

MIDDLE STONE

DARK EARTH

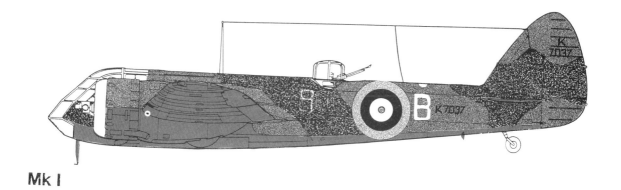

Mk I

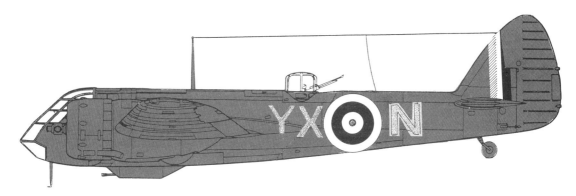

Mk I F

MEDITERRANEAN
BLUE

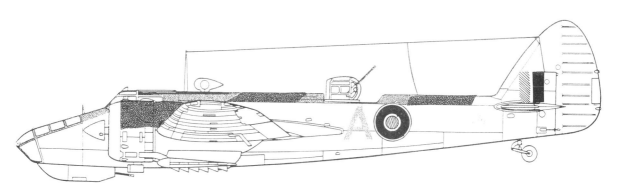

Mk V

The Bristol Beaufighter

Utilising the experience gained in the design and production of the reasonably successful Blenheim and the somewhat less successful Beaufort, the Bristol Aeroplane Company launched a private venture to supply a heavy escort/night fighter replacement.

Basing the new aircraft mainly on the strong but underpowered Beaufort, they married the rear fuselage, undercarriage and wings to a new nose. The first flight took place in July 1939, with deliveries commencing in almost exactly a year and the type beginning operations the following September. The powerful, two-seater proved an excellent airframe to carry the AI airborne radio detection equipment, and the aircraft was quickly substituted in place of the inadequate Blenheim and Defiant types then used in the nocturnal role. The 'Beau' operated successfully as a night fighter, until it was itself superseded by the excellent Mosquito.

Meanwhile, the type was developed for the role for which it was originally intended, where its great power and heavy standard armament of four cannon and six machine guns – which made it the most heavily-armed fighter of its day – proved devastating, and these were progressively augmented by rocket and torpedo weapons.

The type was extensively used in North Africa, where extra fuel tanks were fitted in the wings at the expense of the six machine guns, and also in the Mediterranean and the Far East, where it replaced the wooden Mosquito whose airframe deteriorated rapidly in the tropical conditions. The three-view drawing shows the aircraft in a typical finish of Dark Sea Grey upper surfaces over Sky undersides and bearing the distinctive black and white 'D Day' invasion stripes.

The top of the side view shows the aircraft in the initial night fighter, smooth, Black overall finish, while the second view shows the Merlin engine Mark II which was introduced as an insurance against the failure of Hercules engine production to keep up with the airframe production. The third view shows the type in the revised night fighter scheme of Dark Green disruption over Medium Sea Grey. The final view depicts a T.F. Mk X Torpedo bomber version.

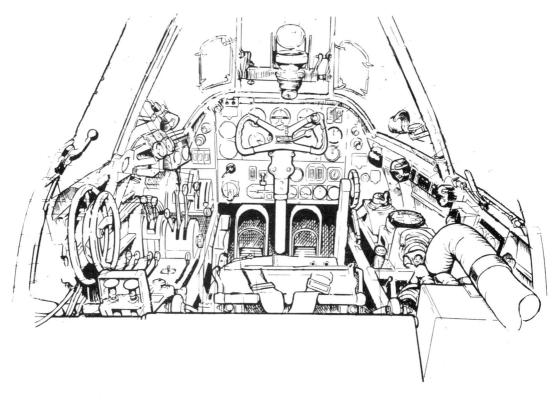

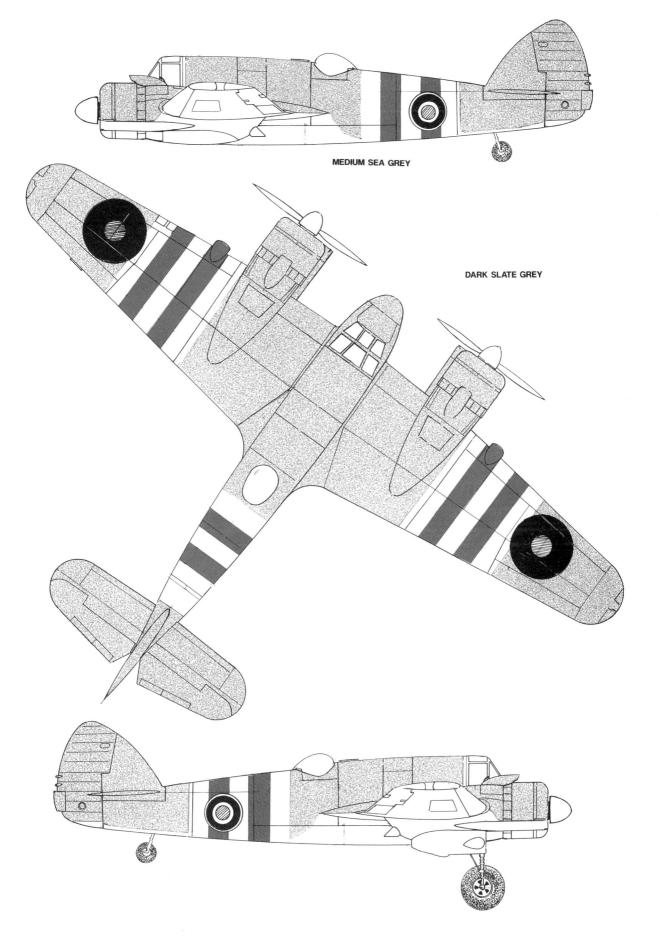

MEDIUM SEA GREY

DARK SLATE GREY

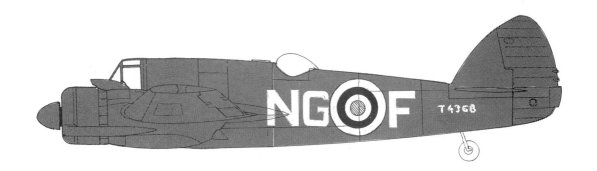

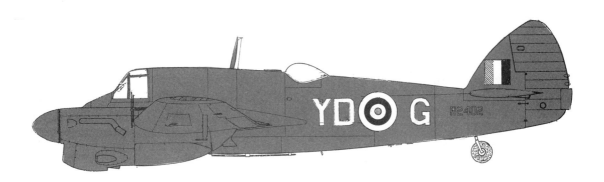

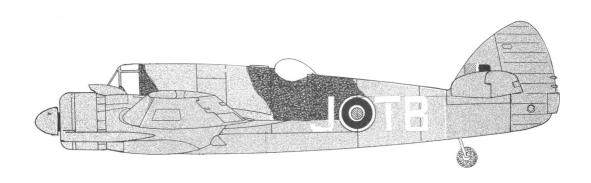

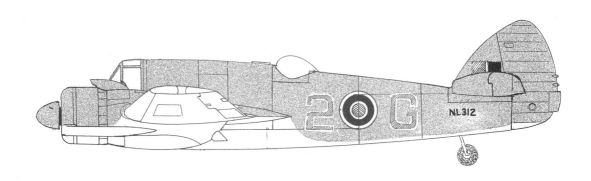

Vickers Wellington

The Wellington bomber was probably the greatest contribution made by the aeronautical design genius Sir Barnes Wallis, who had previously designed the very successful R100 airship and Wellesley long-range monoplane bomber. He is better remembered for his work on the bouncing and earthquake bombs used by the RAF during the War.

In his design for the Wellington, Wallis used his well-proven 'geodetic' basketweave framework covered in fabric for both fuselage and wings which gave the aircraft great strength and integrity, even when severely damaged by enemy action, a quality which endeared it to its crews. The aircraft bore the brunt of the British bombing offensive until gradually replaced by the four-engined Halifax and Lancaster bombers in late 1942 and through 1943. The type was also extensively used by Coastal Command carrying not only radio location and detection equipment, later named RADAR by the Americans, but also a Leigh light searchlight for illuminating the target at night, and requiring the aircraft to patrol at 500ft for long periods.

Once again, the three-view drawing gives a representation of the initial standard bomber scheme of Dark Green and Dark Earth on the top surfaces, and the fuselage sides with undersides in smooth Black. Before hostilities, these would bear the aircraft serial number in large white numbers and letters. The top side view is a Mk 1, with its distinctive Vickers gun turrets and bold squadron markings and serial numbers combined with 'B' type national markings, as seen during the 'phoney war' over the winter of 1939/40.

The second view of a Mk 1C is included to show the quite common Bomber Command modification of the national insignia which, during 1941/42, the white was either dulled down significantly or painted out with Black. However, this move does seem to have been compromised by retaining the broad yellow outline and Light Grey squadron codes! This aircraft is from 311 Czechoslovakian Squadron, the only squadron representing this nation in Bomber Command.

The third view shows a Wellington XII serving in Coastal Command, and finished in the Grey/Green top colours with White undersides extending well up the fuselage sides, and fitted with the ASV MKIII radar housed in the fairing under the nose.

The final view is of a MK IV aircraft, a type which was built at the same time as the MK III, but had American Pratt & Whitney R.1830-53C4-G engines, introduced as a safeguard against the loss of British engine manufacturing capacity through enemy action. This aircraft was, in fact, re-covered and used to augment the inadequate RAF transport services in India.

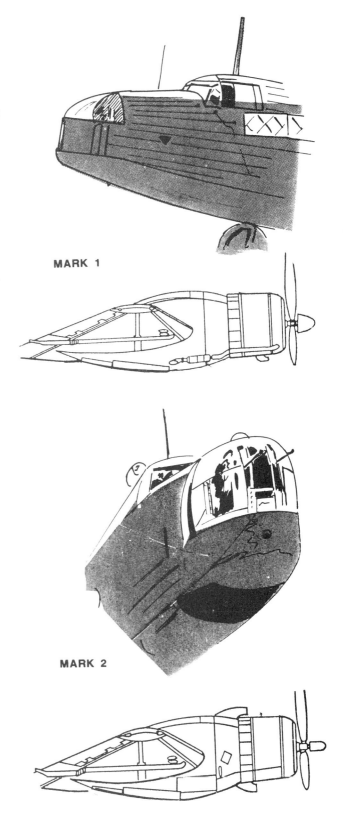

MARK 1

MARK 2

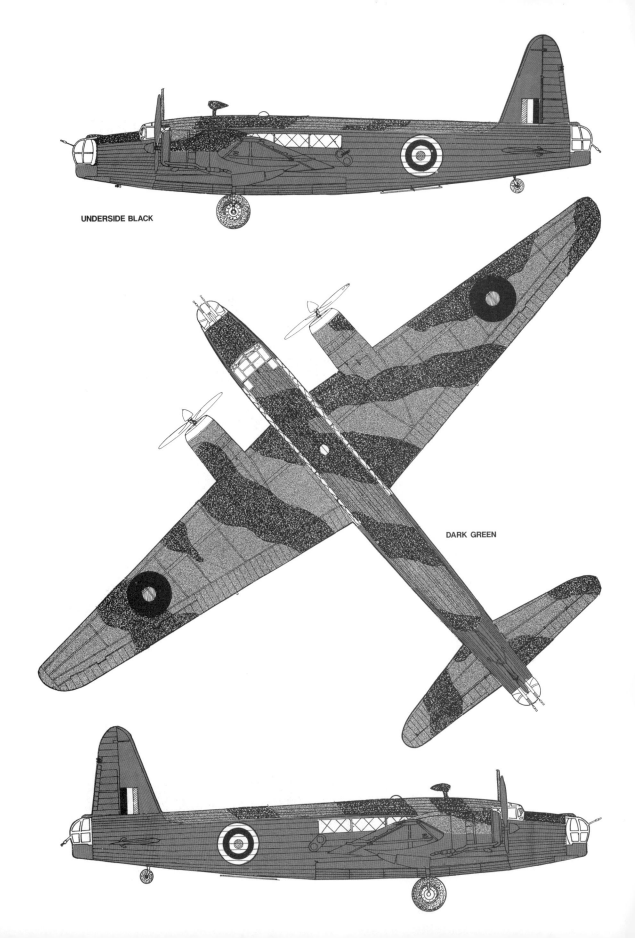

UNDERSIDE BLACK

DARK GREEN

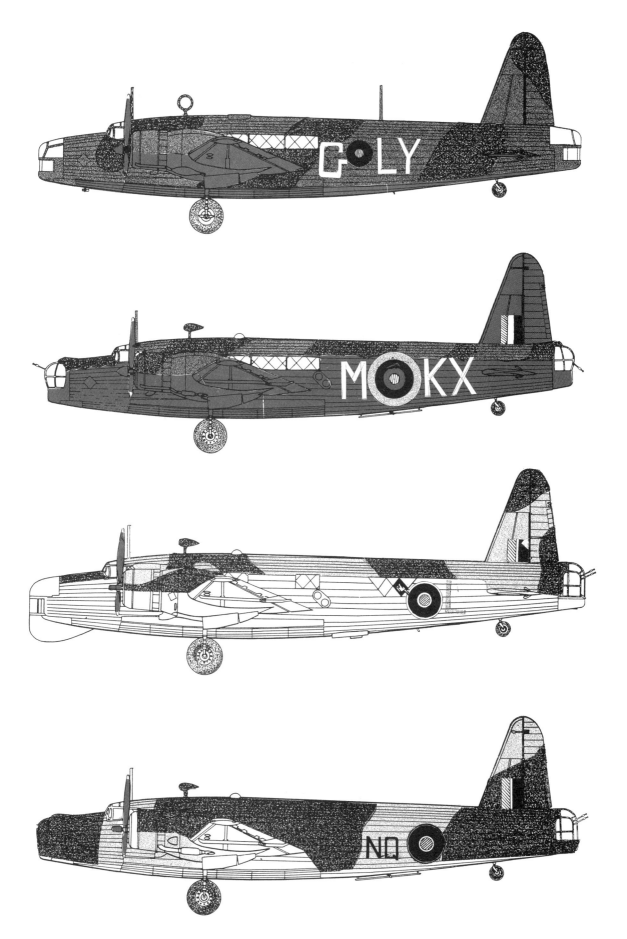

Hawker Typhoon/Tempest

Shortly after the introduction of the Hurricane, it became evident that development of its more traditional type of airframe construction would be limited. In 1937 the Hawker design team undertook designing a replacement, powered either by the new Vulture or Sabre engines. Continuous problems caused abandonment of the former, the latter appearing in February 1940 as the Typhoon. This in turn was also experiencing engine installation problems and the type did not enter service until September the following year, but engine problems still dominated the types' reputation.

At high speed, and with a superficial resemblance to its FW190 opponent, the Typhoon became subject to an alarmingly large number of mistaken identity attacks which resulted in the Black/White identity bands, applied initially right round the wings and later on the bottom wing surfaces only. These should not be confused with the similar but subsequent 'D' day markings applied to all Allied types which were of equal width bands. The specialised Typhoon markings are shown in the three view drawing.

The Typhoon was able to create its niche in history, however, as the RAF's ground attack fighter - when armed with cannon and rocket it decimated German army units in France during the 'D' Day operation and subsequent advance. In an attempt to rectify the shortcomings of the Typhoon, Hawkers submitted a redesign of the basic airframe this time with thin elliptical wings. This amendment evolved as the more successful Tempest.

The top side view shows one of the initial batch of aircraft with the early 'Solid' rear end to the cockpit and before the application of the Black/White recognition markings. Side view two shows the later style canopy of the aircraft serving with 56 Squadron, the first unit to operate the type.

The third view shows a Tempest V of No 3 Squadron which was mainly deployed in intercepting the V1 flying bombs.

The final view shows the Mk II variant in post-War markings as this variant was delayed in entering service due to engine development problems.

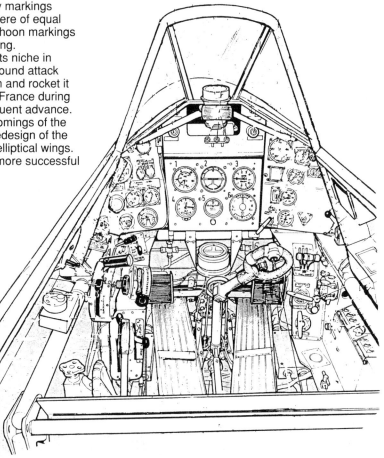

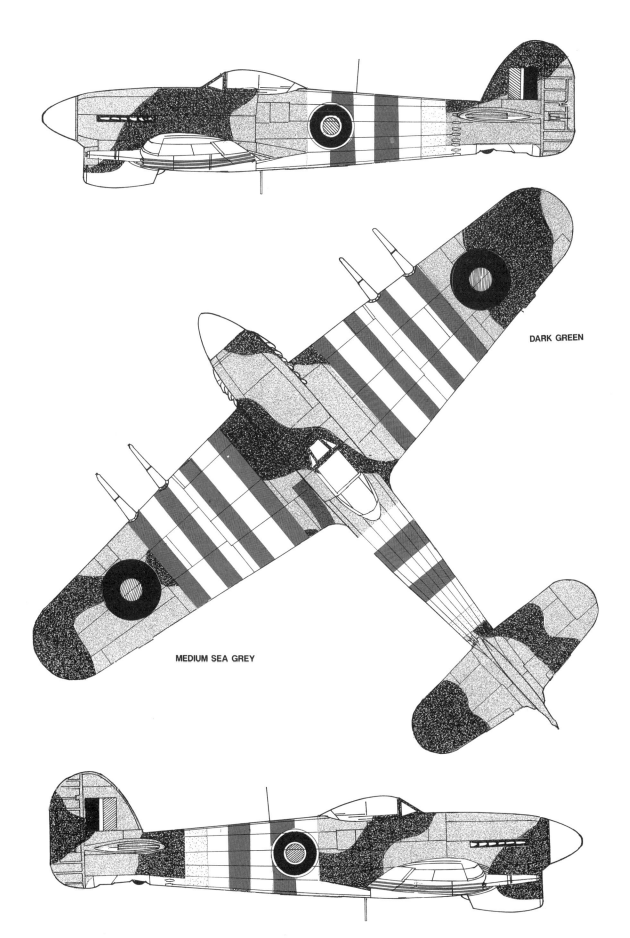

DARK GREEN

MEDIUM SEA GREY

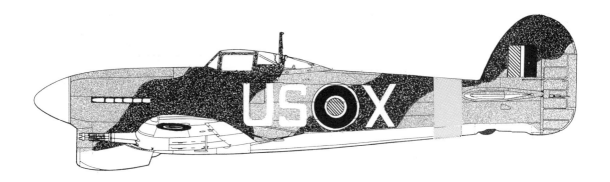

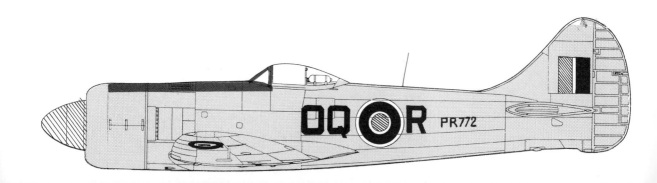

The De Havilland Mosquito

The Mosquito was the finest and most versatile combat aircraft to emerge during the Second World War. Its concept as an unarmed, high level bomber, built from non-strategic wood, produced an outstanding performance.

The first to go into service were in the photo reconnaissance role in September 1941. The bomber variant, the Mk IV, followed into action in the November of that year, and soon gained a reputation, with both the RAF and the Luftwaffe, by striking deep into enemy territory with great accuracy and almost complete immunity. Its performance rapidly led to the development of a night fighter derivative – the NFII – which entered service in early 1942, supplementing, and finally replacing, the Beaufighter. Further development took place in all three major variants – the aircraft operating from tree-top height to an altitude of 40,000ft. BOAC utilised it for executive (albeit somewhat uncomfortable) transport to the neutral countries. Coastal Command also acquired the type for long-range operations against the enemy.

The bomber variant underwent constant improvement, which introduced a pressurised cabin allowing the type to operate at ever-increasing altitude, and raising the bomb load from the original four 250lb bombs to 4000lb which could be carried as a single weapon.

The three views show a fighter variant finished in the overall Fighter Grey with a disruptive pattern in Dark Green on the top surfaces and sides. This basic pattern would be the same for other top surface colour combinations.

The top side view shows an NF II Night Fighter in a black finish which initially was the velvet black texture but was soon amended to a smooth eggshell finish.

The second view is that of the early day bomber finish of Dark Earth/Dark Green top with Sky undersides.

The third view is again of a Night Fighter. This time the NF10 with its enlarged nose and bearing standard Grey/Dark Green top with a black underside which was used during the 1943-44 period.

The final side view shows the Mosquito in its other major role, that of photo reconnaissance aircraft in overall PRU Blue and Red/Blue national markings, white lettering and airframe serial.

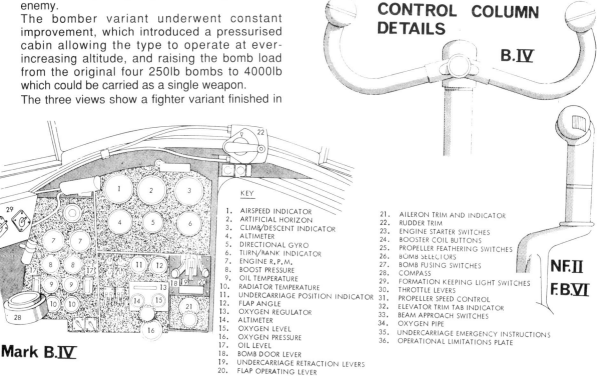

CONTROL COLUMN DETAILS

B.IV

NF.II

F.B.VI

KEY

1. AIRSPEED INDICATOR
2. ARTIFICIAL HORIZON
3. CLIMB/DESCENT INDICATOR
4. ALTIMETER
5. DIRECTIONAL GYRO
6. TURN/BANK INDICATOR
7. ENGINE R.P.M.
8. BOOST PRESSURE
9. OIL TEMPERATURE
10. RADIATOR TEMPERATURE
11. UNDERCARRIAGE POSITION INDICATOR
12. FLAP ANGLE
13. OXYGEN REGULATOR
14. ALTIMETER
15. OXYGEN LEVEL
16. OXYGEN PRESSURE
17. OIL LEVEL
18. BOMB DOOR LEVER
19. UNDERCARRIAGE RETRACTION LEVERS
20. FLAP OPERATING LEVER
21. AILERON TRIM AND INDICATOR
22. RUDDER TRIM
23. ENGINE STARTER SWITCHES
24. BOOSTER COIL BUTTONS
25. PROPELLER FEATHERING SWITCHES
26. BOMB SELECTORS
27. BOMB FUSING SWITCHES
28. COMPASS
29. FORMATION KEEPING LIGHT SWITCHES
30. THROTTLE LEVERS
31. PROPELLER SPEED CONTROL
32. ELEVATOR TRIM TAB INDICATOR
33. BEAM APPROACH SWITCHES
34. OXYGEN PIPE
35. UNDERCARRIAGE EMERGENCY INSTRUCTIONS
36. OPERATIONAL LIMITATIONS PLATE

Mark B.IV

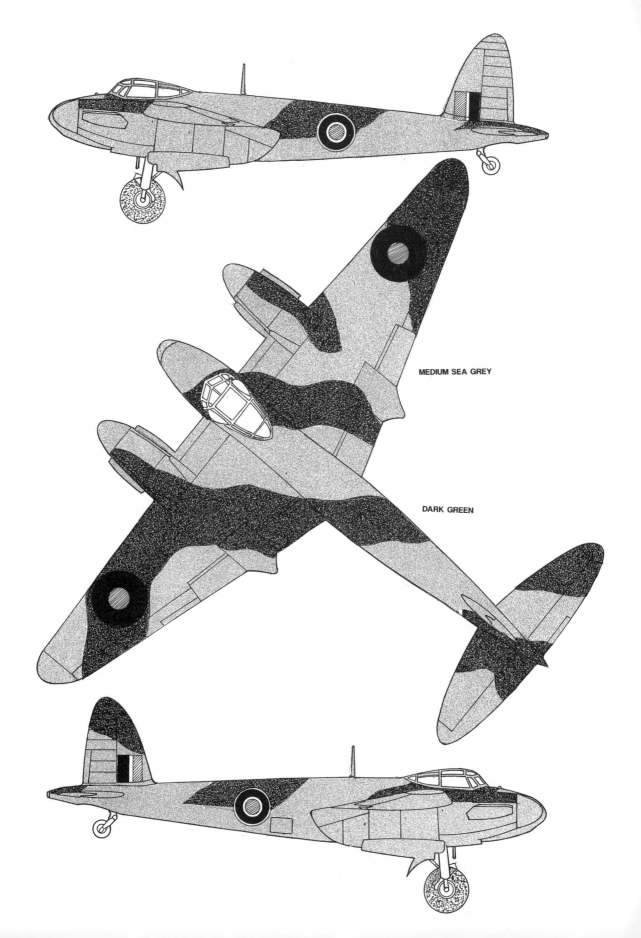

MEDIUM SEA GREY

DARK GREEN

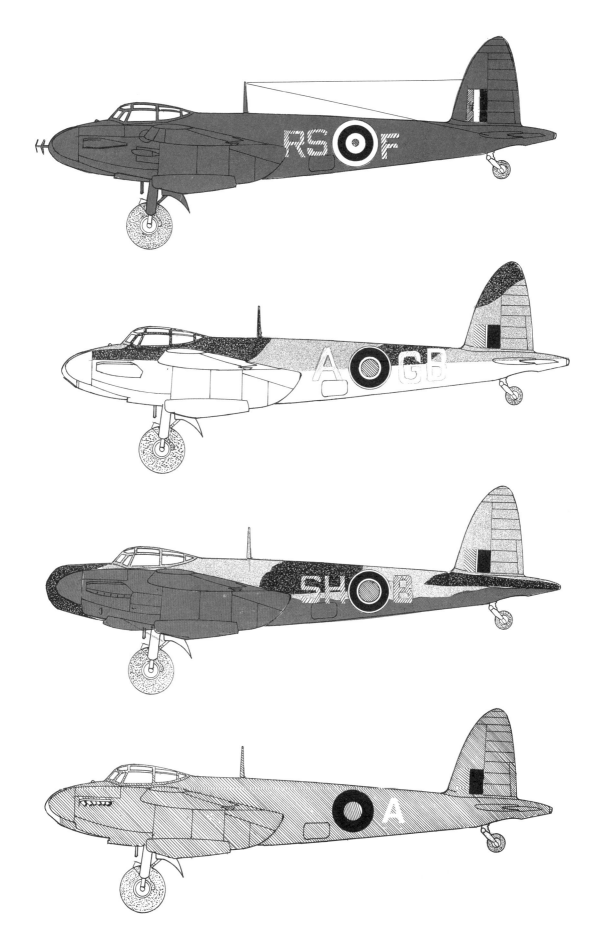

The Avro Lancaster

The Lancaster was, without doubt, the most outstanding heavy bomber of the War.

It evolved from an unsuccessful twin-engine type, the Manchester, which had the unenviable reputation of suffering more losses through engine failure than enemy action! Roy Chadwick and his team, realising the excellence of the basic design, decided to replace the two troublesome Vulture engines with four of the now available and proven Merlin engines. They took the opportunity to increase the wing span from 90'1" to 102', a move which greatly improved the aircraft's operational service ceiling.

Its performance and exploits became legendary, as it increased its bomb load from an initial 4,000lb up to the full 10 tons (22,000lb). Accommodated in one large bomb bay, this enabled more devastating larger types of bombs to be used than other types were able to carry (the B17's standard load was six 1,600lb armour piercing bombs). It also, of course, carried out the famous Dams Raid, but its nightly intrusions into occupied Europe's airspace remain its great contribution to the British and Commonwealth war effort.

The three views show the basic Bomber Command camouflage scheme, generally applicable to all four-engine heavy bombers.

The top view gives a good example of a squadron anomaly in marking, with both the squadron ident PH and the individual letter being applied aft of the national marking as applied by 12 Squadron based at Wickenby during 1943.

The second view shows the more standard markings, this time for an aircraft of 101 Squadron equipped with the airborne signal jamming radio equipment, shown by the two large aerials on top of the fuselage.

The third view is one of the famous Dams Raid aircraft of 617 Squadron, without which it seems no reference to the 'Lanc' is complete.

The fourth side view shows the basic markings modified for daylight use, and with Yellow outlines to the side lettering and coloured fins and rudders of a flight leader from 617 Squadron.

LANCASTER FLAP DETAIL

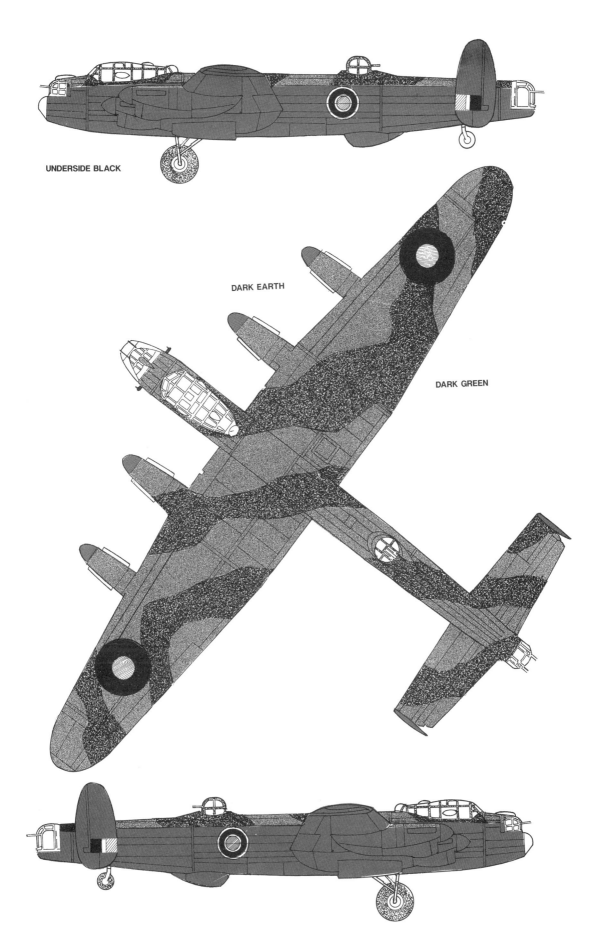

UNDERSIDE BLACK

DARK EARTH

DARK GREEN

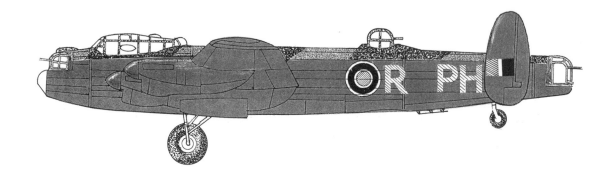

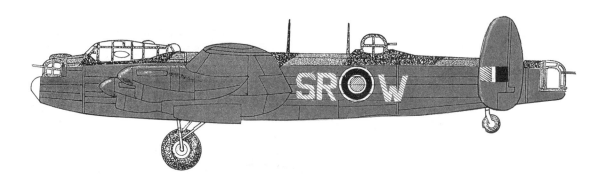

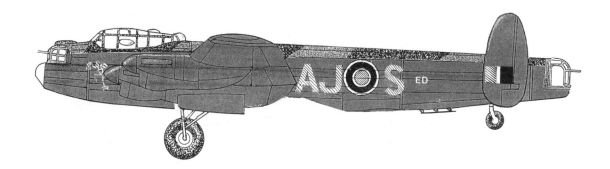

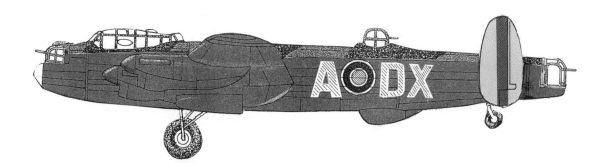

Short Sunderland

When the design team at Short proposed a military version of their C class flying boat, they cannot have envisaged it would have a 35-year career, nor that it would make a vital contribution to the survival of the British Isles.

In the early War years, the Sunderland was responsible for the major part of anti-U-boat air protection to the vital supply convoys during the first phase of the Battle of the Atlantic.

The Sunderland could also 'take care of itself', being more than capable of seeing off the Fw200 Condor which was used for reconnaissance for the German U-boat submarine packs searching for the vulnerable merchant convoys.

It is also recorded, on more than one occasion, to have taken on packs of Ju88 long-range fighters and emerged triumphant having downed a number of its assailants. The type is also responsible for the first rescue of shipwrecked seamen, when two Sunderlands picked up the survivors of the torpedoed steamer *Kensington Court* in a stormy mid-ocean.

The three-view drawing shows the map pattern camouflage which was originally applied in Dark Earth/Dark Green/Sky colours. However, it soon became obvious that this was not suitable and it was quickly replaced by Grey-Green upper surfaces, being retrospectively applied to earlier aircraft at major overhauls. These aircraft were worked hard and long with great periods of monotonous patrols and few interceptions of enemy aircraft or submarines.

Side view one shows a Mk1 Sunderland in the Grey-Green finish. The Mark II, shown in view two and introduced in August 1941, shows the power turret introduced on the 15th production example of this mark replacing the dorsal side guns and having more powerful engines.

The third side view shows the MkIII variant, the most important and prolific mark, with the revised colours introduced in August 1942 when White was applied to the undersides and well up the sides, sometimes with an irregular edge. Note the change in shape to the hull bottom, the original step being eliminated.

Our final view shows a Mark V aircraft which had American engines of greater power repressing some of the loss of performance caused by increasing all up weights. Late in the War, some aircraft appeared with plain Grey top surfaces.

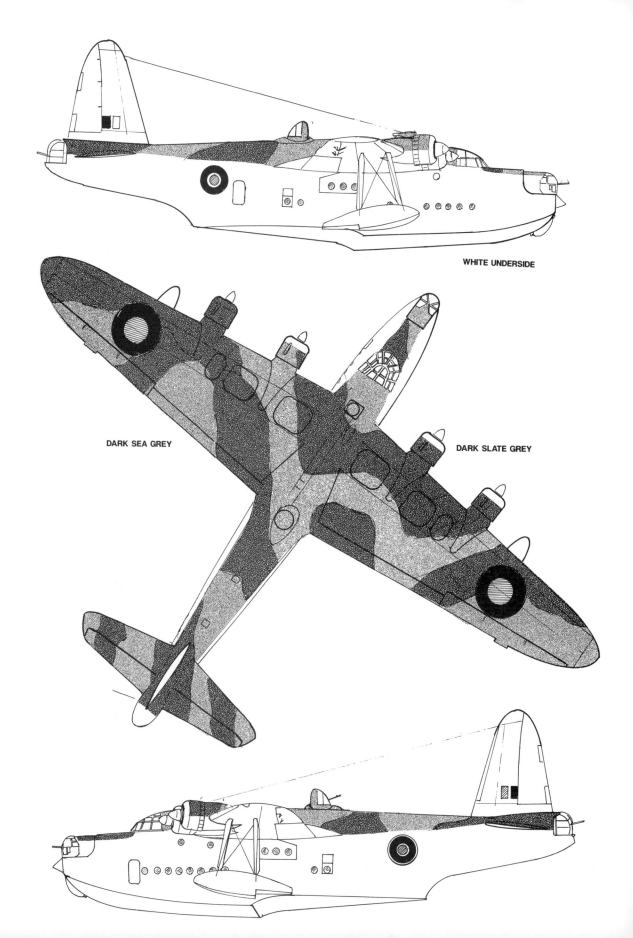

WHITE UNDERSIDE

DARK SEA GREY

DARK SLATE GREY

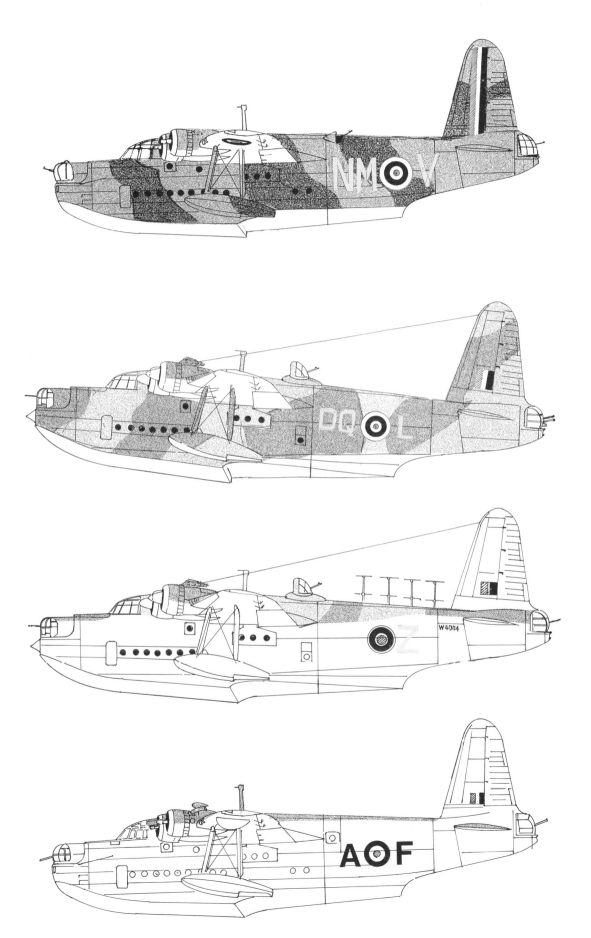

Gloster Meteor

While the Meteor cannot be regarded in the same category as the classic fighters and bombers, its inclusion in this book is quite justified.

So far as the RAF is concerned, it is the last link in the wartime chain of aircraft development that started with a 90mph biplane owing much of its design to an earlier conflict, and ended with the present Jet Age.

Conservatism and lack of interest in both Britain and Germany delayed the introduction of jet-powered aircraft into service for some time, and the Meteor, with its high speed at low altitude, was really only brought into service in July 1944 to combat the V1 Flying Bomb onslaught. It saw no other air combat, although by the end of the War three squadrons had been equipped with the type.

Therefore, the outcome of any combat between the Meteor and the Me 262a, Germany's main jet fighter type, can only be speculation. However, although the British aircraft had sound construction and more reliable engines, it lacked the German machine's refined aerodynamics. But its sound basic design allowed the type to become Fighter Command's mainstay for a number of years.

It was developed through a number of variants, ending with a number of two-seat night fighter types with elongated noses carrying large radar units. This development finally cured the tail heavy C of G problem that had plagued the Meteor (and many other early jet designs) for most of their lives.

The three-view drawing shows how little the basic camouflage pattern introduced at the beginning of the War needed to be changed to accommodate the new breed of fighter. Indeed, the same pattern, but more modified, would be applied to the later swept-wing Hunter and Swift aircraft.

The top view shows the prototype bearing the significant Yellow P in a circle on the fuselage and in a Green/Earth finish with Yellow undersides.

The second view shows one of the earliest Mk1s in service against the V1, and operating with 616(F) Squadron from RAF Manston.

View three shows a Mk3 serving with 222 (NATAL) Squadron in late 1945 and, having a gloss finish, while the final view shows a modified F3 in Naval service with 793NAS at Ford in 1950.

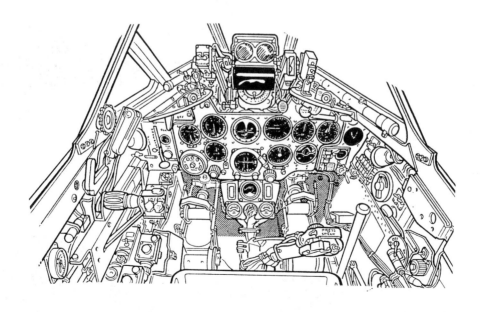

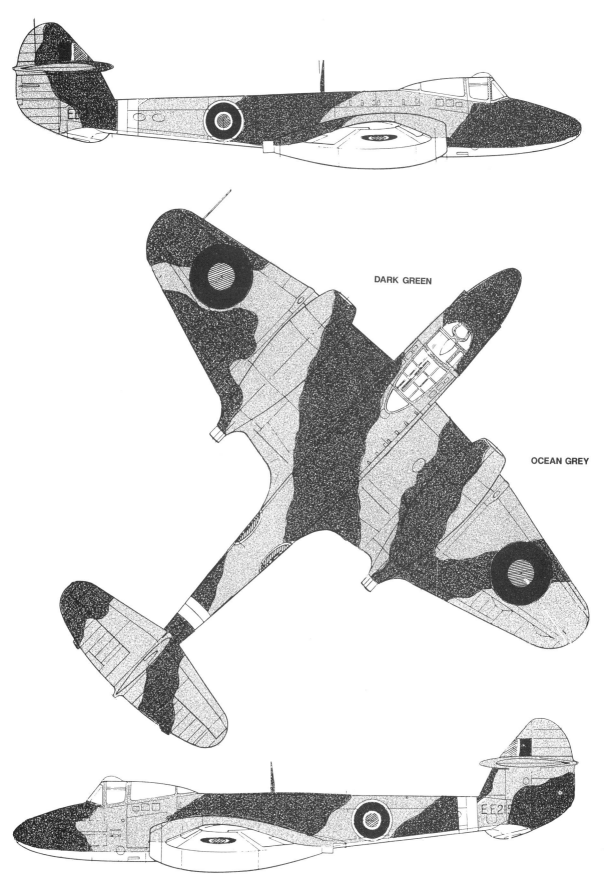

DARK GREEN

OCEAN GREY

MEDIUM SEA GREY

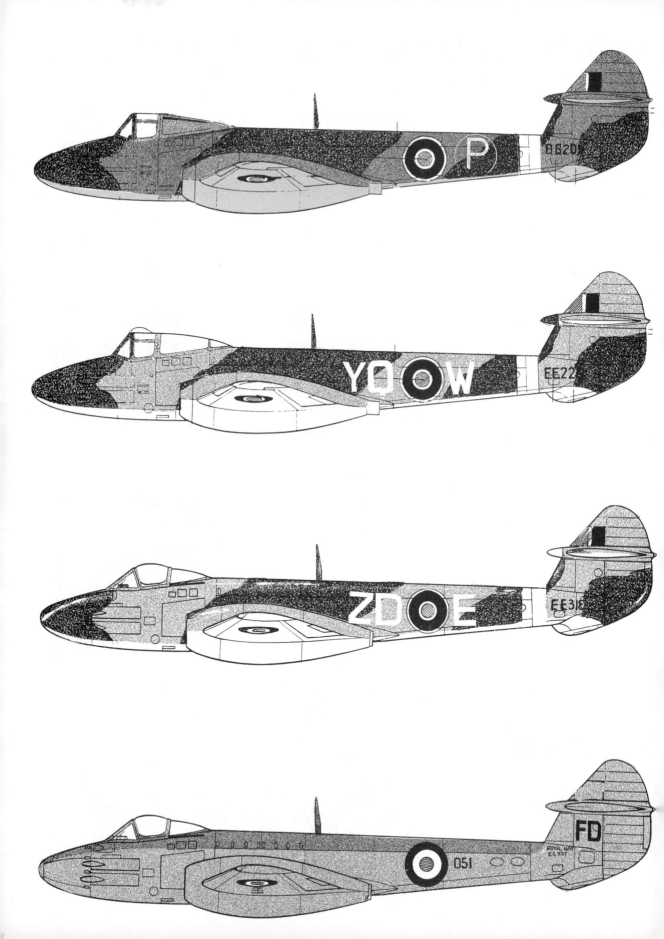